Anima

by Nicholas Spencer
illustrated by Anna Jones

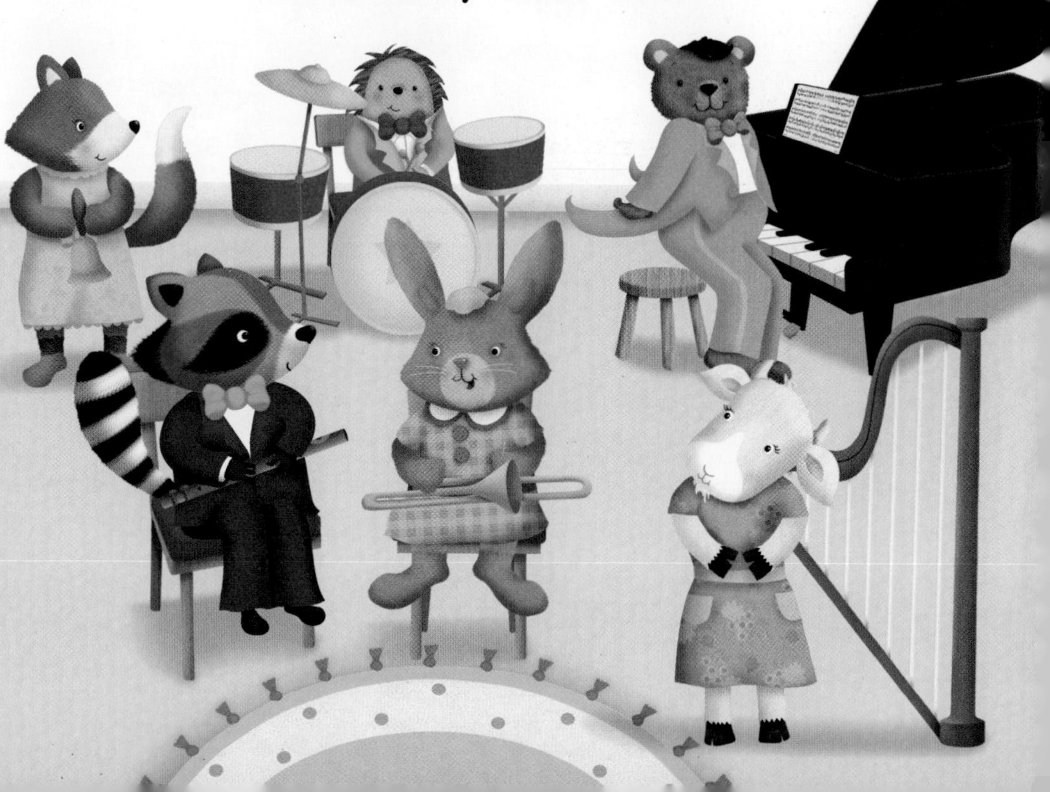

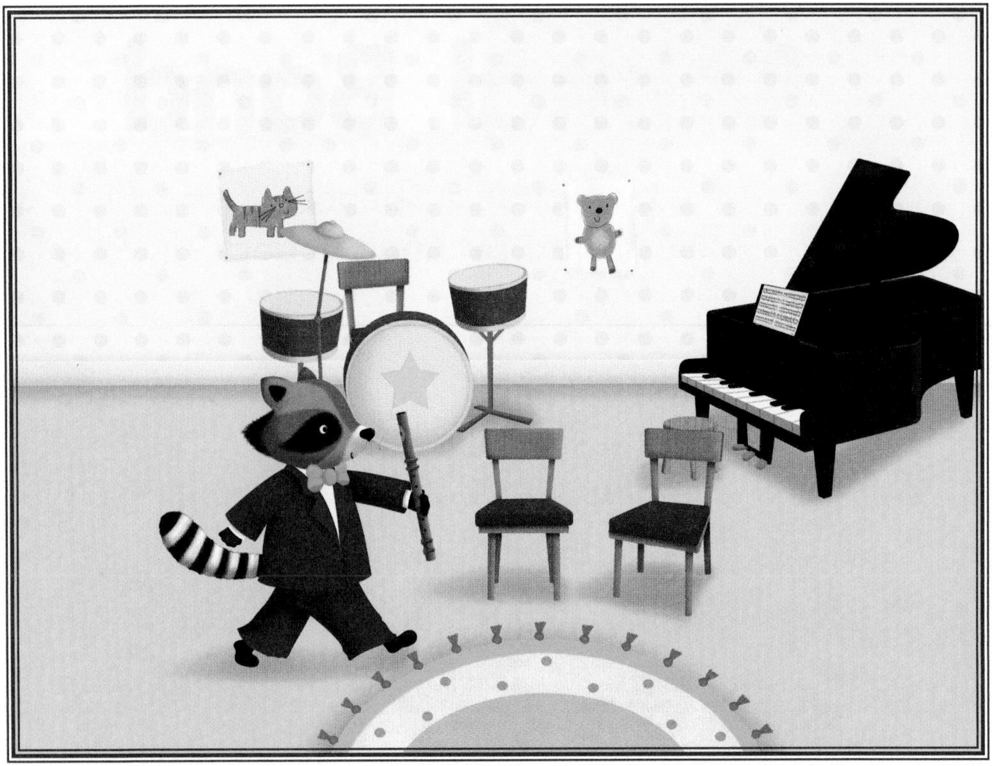

The flute is good.

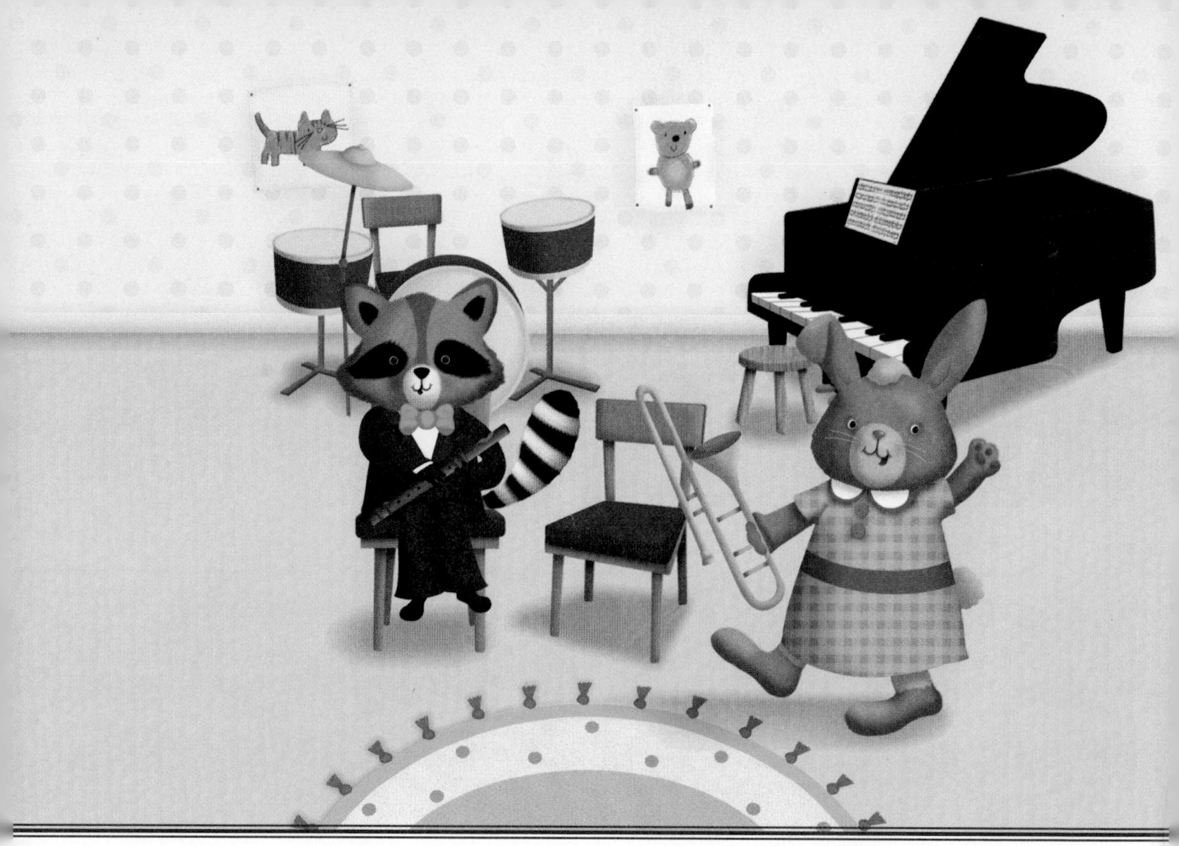

The horn is good.

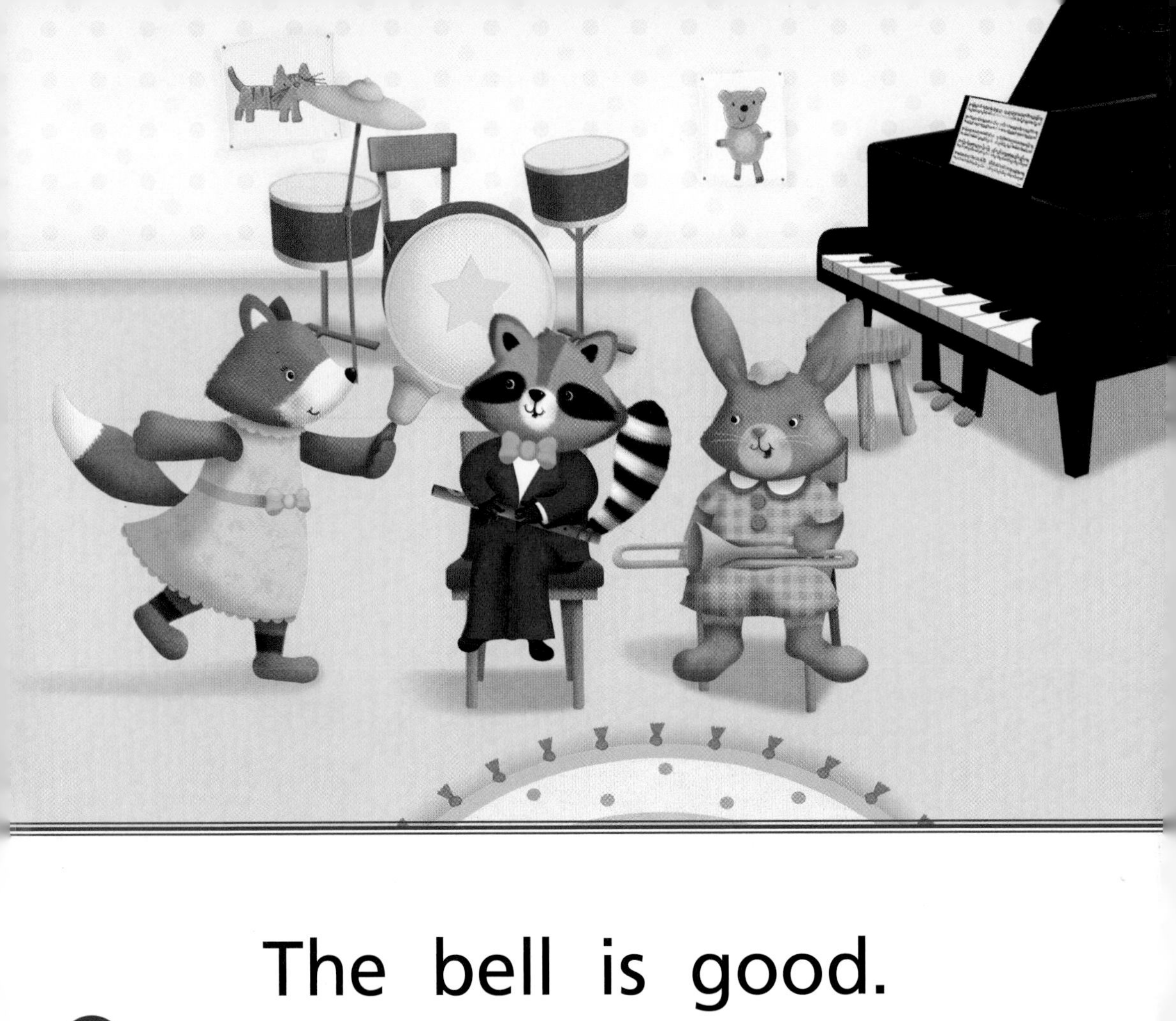

The bell is good.

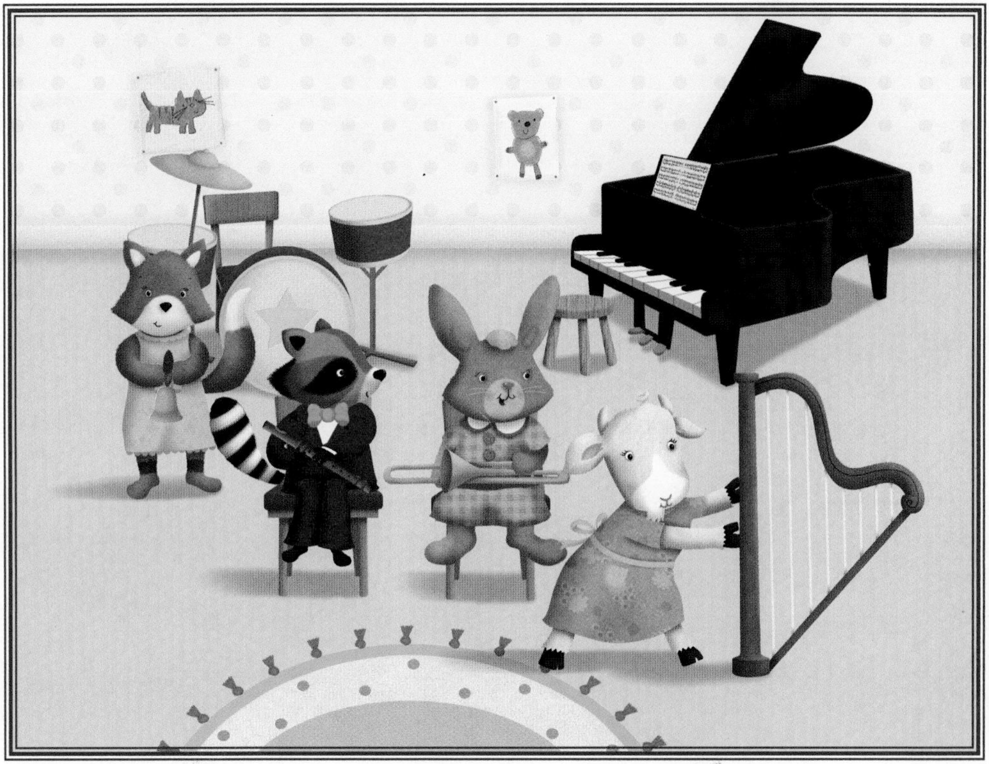

The harp is good.

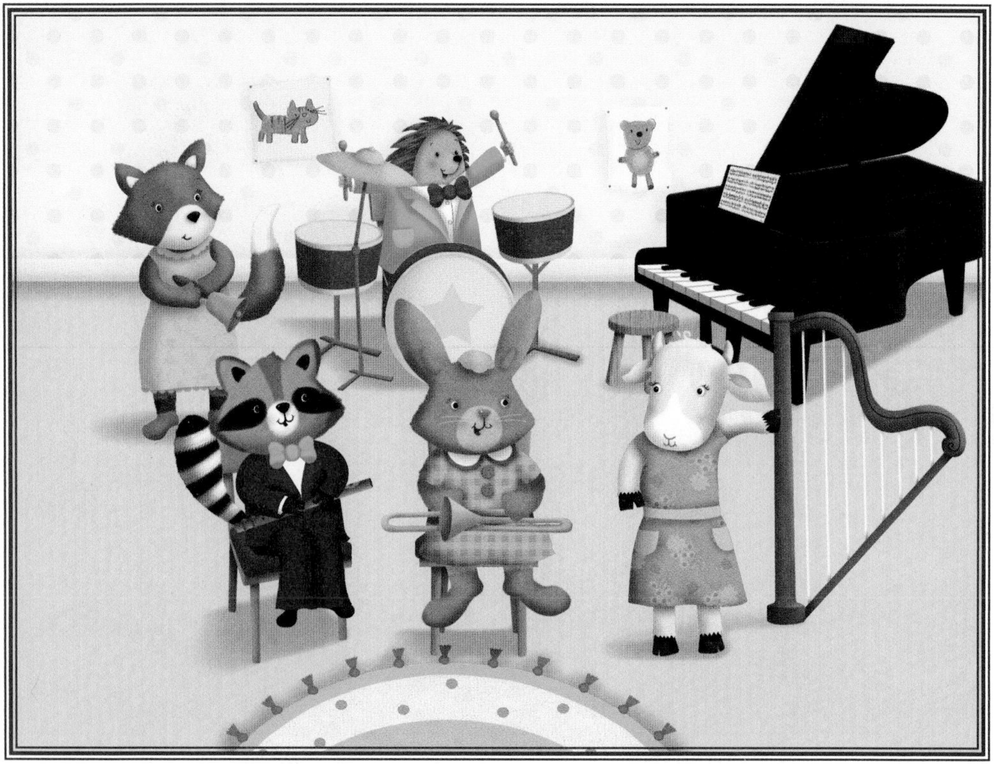

The drum is good.

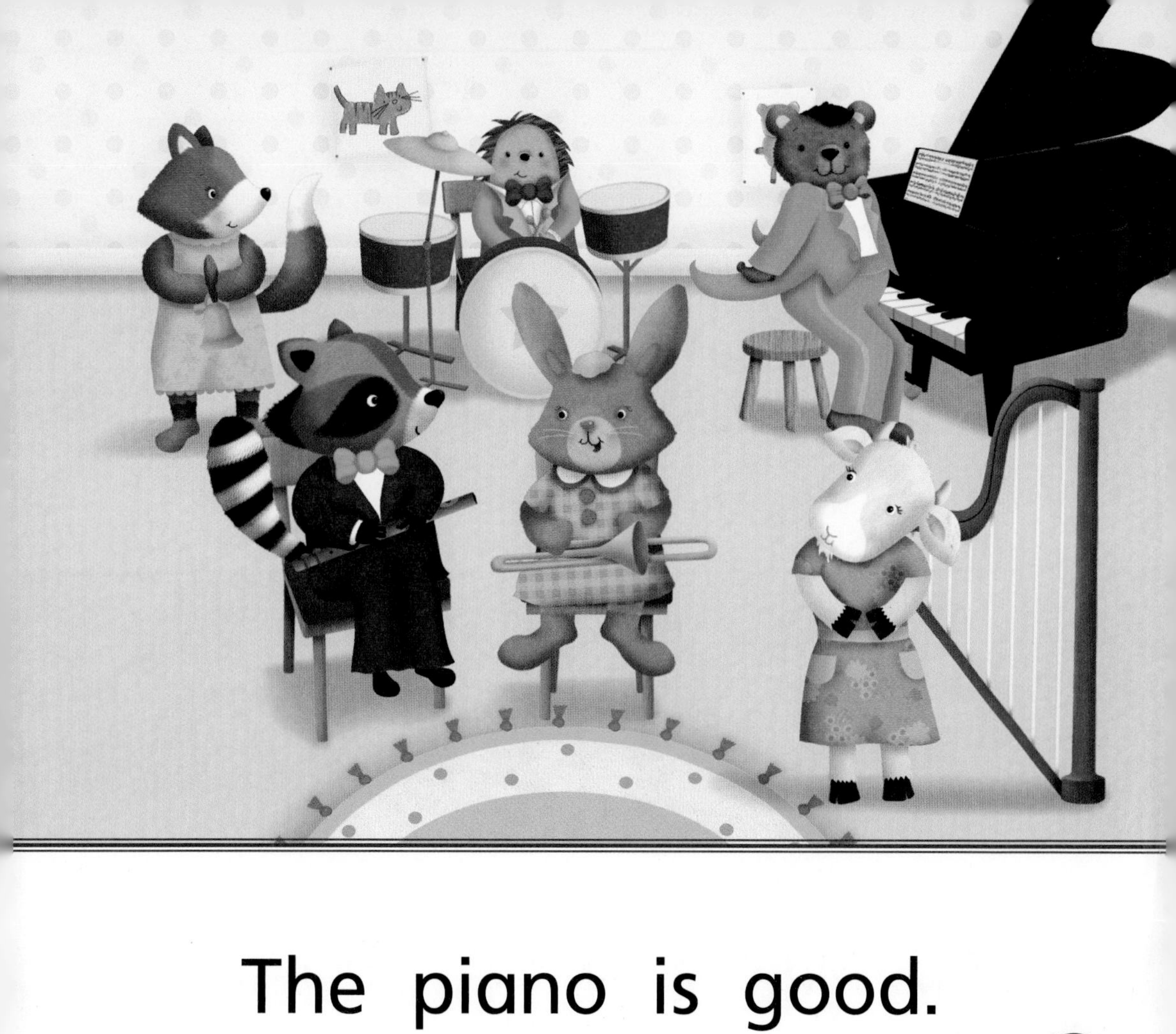

The piano is good.

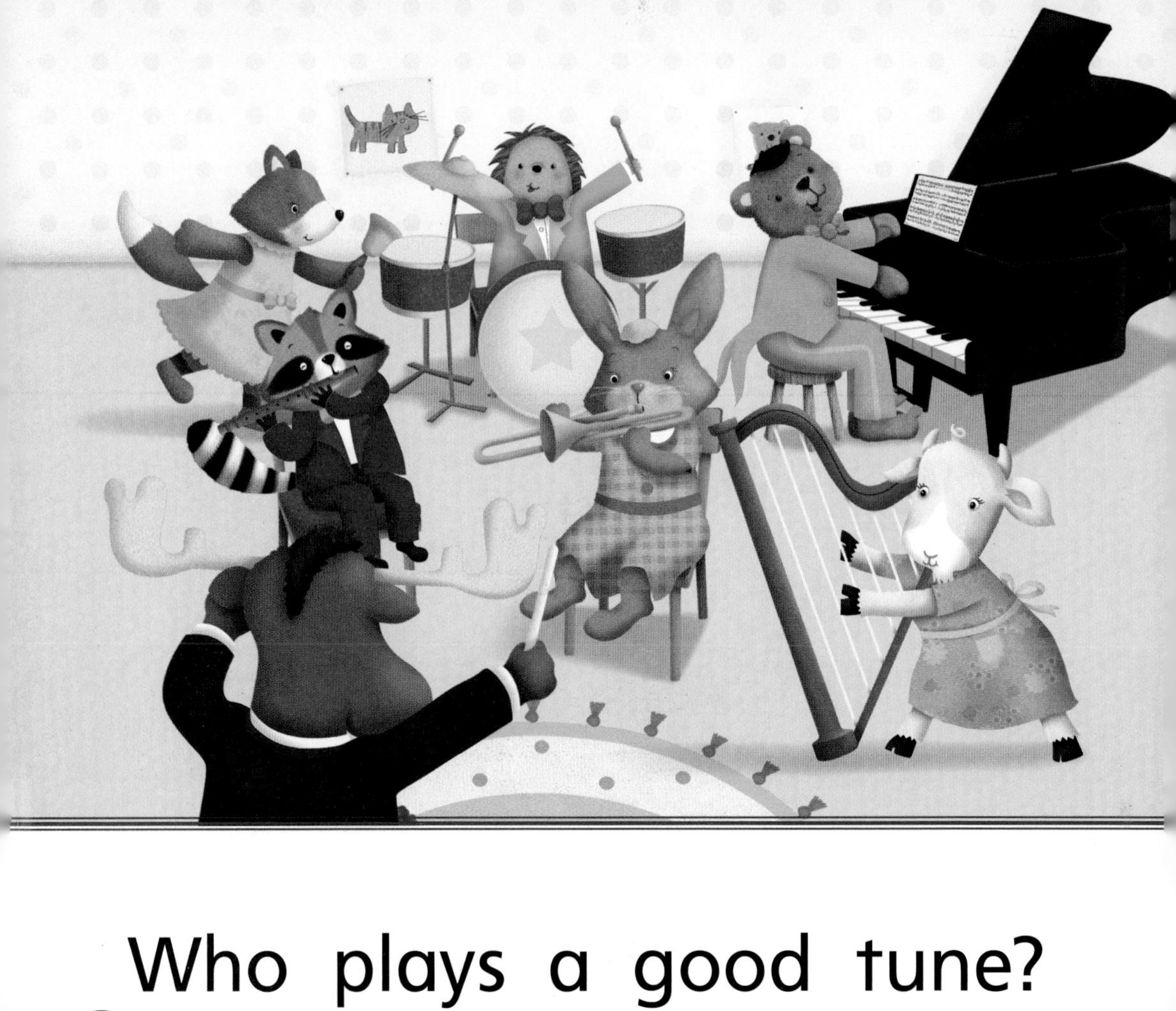

Who plays a good tune?